# FAMILY GUY™

# MAD LIBS®

By Roger Price and Leonard Stern

PSS!

PRICE STERN SLOAN

W9-BGM-164

PRICE STERN SLOAN
Published by the Penguin Group
Penguin Group (USA) Inc., 375 Hudson Street, New York, New York 10014, USA
Penguin Group (Canada), 90 Eglinton Avenue East, Suite 700,
Toronto, Ontario, Canada M4P 2Y3
(a division of Pearson Penguin Canada Inc.)
Penguin Books Ltd, 80 Strand, London WC2R 0RL, England
Penguin Ireland, 25 St Stephen's Green, Dublin 2, Ireland (a division of Penguin Books Ltd)
Penguin Group (Australia), 250 Camberwell Road, Camberwell, Victoria 3124, Australia
(a division of Pearson Australia Group Pty Ltd)
Penguin Books India Pvt Ltd, 11 Community Centre,
Panchsheel Park, New Delhi-110 017, India
Penguin Group (NZ), Cnr Airborne and Rosedale Roads,
Albany, Auckland 1310, New Zealand (a division of Pearson New Zealand Ltd)
Penguin Books (South Africa) (Pty) Ltd, 24 Sturdee Avenue,
Rosebank, Johannesburg 2196, South Africa

Penguin Books Ltd, Registered Offices: 80 Strand, London WC2R 0RL, England

Published by Price Stern Sloan,
a division of Penguin Young Readers Group,
345 Hudson Street, New York, New York 10014.

ISBN 978-0-8431-2190-2

3  5  7  9  10  8  6  4  2

# MAD LIBS®

## INSTRUCTIONS

MAD LIBS® is a game for people who don't like games!
It can be played by one, two, three, four, or forty.

### • RIDICULOUSLY SIMPLE DIRECTIONS

In this tablet you will find stories containing blank spaces where words are left out. One player, the READER, selects one of these stories. The READER does not tell anyone what the story is about. Instead, he/she asks the other players, the WRITERS, to give him/her words. These words are used to fill in the blank spaces in the story.

### • TO PLAY

The READER asks each WRITER in turn to call out a word—an adjective or a noun or whatever the space calls for—and uses them to fill in the blank spaces in the story. The result is a MAD LIBS® game.

When the READER then reads the completed MAD LIBS® game to the other players, they will discover that they have written a story that is fantastic, screamingly funny, shocking, silly, crazy, or just plain dumb—depending upon which words each WRITER called out.

### • EXAMPLE (Before and After)

" _____!" he said _____
         EXCLAMATION                              ADVERB

as he jumped into his convertible _____ and
                                                    NOUN

drove off with his _____ wife.
                              ADJECTIVE

" _____Ouch_____!" he said _____stupidly_____
         EXCLAMATION                              ADVERB

as he jumped into his convertible _____cat_____ and
                                                    NOUN

drove off with his _____brave_____ wife.
                              ADJECTIVE

# MAD LIBS®

## QUICK REVIEW

In case you have forgotten what adjectives, adverbs, nouns, and verbs are, here is a quick review:

An ADJECTIVE describes something or somebody. *Lumpy, soft, ugly, messy,* and *short* are adjectives.

An ADVERB tells how something is done. It modifies a verb and usually ends in "ly." *Modestly, stupidly, greedily,* and *carefully* are adverbs.

A NOUN is the name of a person, place, or thing. *Sidewalk, umbrella, bridle, bathtub,* and *nose* are nouns.

A VERB is an action word. *Run, pitch, jump,* and *swim* are verbs. Put the verbs in past tense if the directions say PAST TENSE. *Ran, pitched, jumped,* and *swam* are verbs in the past tense.

When we ask for A PLACE, we mean any sort of place: a country or city *(Spain, Cleveland)* or a room *(bathroom, kitchen).*

An EXCLAMATION or SILLY WORD is any sort of funny sound, gasp, grunt, or outcry, like *Wow!, Ouch!, Whomp!, Ick!,* and *Gadzooks!*

When we ask for specific words, like a NUMBER, a COLOR, an ANIMAL, or a PART OF THE BODY, we mean a word that is one of those things, like *seven, blue, horse,* or *head*.

When we ask for a PLURAL, it means more than one. For example, *cat* pluralized is *cats*.

MAD LIBS® is fun to play with friends, but you can also play it by yourself! To begin with, DO NOT look at the story on the page below. Fill in the blanks on this page with the words called for. Then, using the words you have selected, fill in the blank spaces in the story.

Now you've created your own hilarious MAD LIBS® game!

# GRIFFIN FAMILY VALUES

PLURAL NOUN _____

ADJECTIVE _____

PLURAL NOUN _____

ADVERB _____

ADJECTIVE _____

NOUN _____

ADVERB _____

PLURAL NOUN _____

ADJECTIVE _____

ADJECTIVE _____

NOUN _____

NOUN _____

ADJECTIVE _____

PART OF THE BODY _____

VERB _____

PLURAL NOUN _____

NOUN _____

NOUN _____

# MAD LIBS®

# GRIFFIN FAMILY VALUES

The Griffins are a family with good old-fashioned American

_____. They may cause a lot of problems, but they
   PLURAL NOUN

always have _____ intentions. And when they behave
              ADJECTIVE

like _____, they _____ admit they're just being
     PLURAL NOUN              ADVERB

_____. When Peter crashes a/an _____ into
   ADJECTIVE                                    NOUN

his neighbor Joe's house, he makes sure to say he is _____
                                                        ADVERB

sorry. And even though Lois has her own _____,
                                           PLURAL NOUN

she tries to be _____ to everyone she meets. When
                 ADJECTIVE

Meg calls Neil a/an _____ _____ on national
                      ADJECTIVE           NOUN

television, she gives him a/an _____ to make up for it.
                                 NOUN

And even though Chris is tormented by a/an _____
                                              ADJECTIVE

monkey, he always turns the other _____. The only
                                    PART OF THE BODY

Griffin who still needs to learn something about how to

_____ in harmony with other _____ is Stewie.
   VERB                                    PLURAL NOUN

He still delights in making a mess on the _____ and
                                             NOUN

blaming it on the _____.
                     NOUN

MAD LIBS® is fun to play with friends, but you can also play it by yourself! To begin with, DO NOT look at the story on the page below. Fill in the blanks on this page with the words called for. Then, using the words you have selected, fill in the blank spaces in the story.

Now you've created your own hilarious MAD LIBS® game!

## MEG'S DIARY

ADVERB _____

NOUN _____

OCCUPATION _____

CELEBRITY_____

PERSON IN ROOM (FEMALE) _____

PART OF THE BODY (PLURAL) _____

A PLACE_____

NOUN _____

PLURAL NOUN_____

PERSON IN ROOM (MALE) _____

EXCLAMATION _____

NOUN _____

NOUN _____

ADJECTIVE _____

NOUN _____

# MAD LIBS®
# MEG'S DIARY

Today was absolutely, positively, _____ the single
                                        ADVERB

worst _____ of my life! First, my dad almost ran over
              NOUN

the school _____ in the parking lot at _____
              OCCUPATION                                CELEBRITY

High. Everybody saw, including _____ and her
                                    PERSON IN ROOM (FEMALE)

friends, and they all rolled their _____ and
                                    PART OF THE BODY (PLURAL)

laughed at me. Now I'll never get to hang out with them at (the)

_____ after school! As if that wasn't embarrassing
        A PLACE

enough, during _____ class, Chris came in and said, "Hey,
                      NOUN

Meg, Mom says not to forget to put your dirty _____
                                                    PLURAL NOUN

in the laundry when you get home because they really stink!"

He said it right in front of _____—the cutest
                              PERSON IN ROOM (MALE)

boy at school! _____! I thought, *Now I'll never*
                  EXCLAMATION

*get a date for the "Moonlight over the* _____*" dance!*
                                              NOUN

Oh diary, I'll have to go to the dance with my _____
                                                        NOUN

and live with my _____ parents forever! My family is
                      ADJECTIVE

ruining my _____!
                NOUN

MAD LIBS® is fun to play with friends, but you can also play it by yourself! To begin with, DO NOT look at the story on the page below. Fill in the blanks on this page with the words called for. Then, using the words you have selected, fill in the blank spaces in the story.

Now you've created your own hilarious MAD LIBS® game!

## STEWIE'S CAMPAIGN SPEECH

PLURAL NOUN _____

NOUN _____

VERB ENDING IN "ING" _____

ADVERB _____

PLURAL NOUN _____

ADJECTIVE _____

NOUN _____

NOUN _____

VERB _____

ADJECTIVE _____

ADJECTIVE _____

PLURAL NOUN _____

NOUN _____

ADJECTIVE _____

PLURAL NOUN _____

NOUN _____

ADJECTIVE _____

PLURAL NOUN _____

# MAD LIBS

# STEWIE'S CAMPAIGN SPEECH

Esteemed ladies and _____, allow me to announce my
                        PLURAL NOUN

candidacy for the position of Supreme _____ of the
                                          NOUN

Universe. I have one year of experience _____ at the
                                        VERB ENDING IN "ING"

Griffin household, where I have _____ managed to
                                      ADVERB

enslave all five family _____. I force the _____
                           PLURAL NOUN                     ADJECTIVE

man to turn the TV on for me each day so I can watch my favorite

program, *The Jolly* _____ *Review*. The one they call
                          NOUN

Meg stays home and _____-sits on Saturday nights while
                          NOUN

the others go out to _____. Chris serves as a guinea
                          VERB

pig upon whom I test my _____ devices. Lois, that
                             ADJECTIVE

_____ woman, cooks my _____, cleans my
    ADJECTIVE                        PLURAL NOUN

_____, and changes my _____ diapers. So
     NOUN                            ADJECTIVE

you see, in just one short year I have taken control of all Griffin

_____. I rule with an iron _____. If elected
  PLURAL NOUN                              NOUN

today, I shall do the same to all of you. I command you to vote for

me, you _____ _____!
         ADJECTIVE        PLURAL NOUN

MAD LIBS® is fun to play with friends, but you can also play it by yourself! To begin with, DO NOT look at the story on the page below. Fill in the blanks on this page with the words called for. Then, using the words you have selected, fill in the blank spaces in the story.

Now you've created your own hilarious MAD LIBS® game!

# PETER'S WORKDAY HEROICS

ADJECTIVE _____

NUMBER_____

ADJECTIVE _____

ADJECTIVE _____

VERB _____

OCCUPATION_____

PLURAL NOUN_____

PLURAL NOUN_____

ADJECTIVE _____

PLURAL NOUN_____

NOUN _____

NOUN _____

ADJECTIVE _____

ADJECTIVE _____

ADJECTIVE _____

NOUN _____

COLOR _____

ADVERB _____

ADJECTIVE _____

# MAD LIBS®
# PETER'S WORKDAY HEROICS

When I used to work at the Happy-Go-_____ toy factory,
                                        ADJECTIVE

I would show up every morning at least _____ minutes
                                         NUMBER

early, _____-eyed and _____-tailed, eager to
        ADJECTIVE              ADJECTIVE

_____. I was a/an _____, which means it was
   VERB                 OCCUPATION

my job to make sure there weren't any metal _____ or
                                              PLURAL NOUN

sharp _____ in the toys. I tell ya, I had a/an _____
       PLURAL NOUN                                   ADJECTIVE

eye for this stuff. I remember the time we manufactured candy

_____ as part of a/an _____'s Day promotion,
 PLURAL NOUN                 NOUN

and I found a/an _____ inside one of the wrappers! I
                  NOUN

knew I had to save all the _____ boys and girls from this
                            ADJECTIVE

_____ menace, so I unwrapped and ate every last piece
 ADJECTIVE

of that _____ candy, thus assuring it would never reach
         ADJECTIVE

_____-store shelves. After I finished, Mr. Weed came by
 NOUN

and his face turned bright _____. "No need to thank me,
                            COLOR

Mr. Weed," I said _____. "I did it for the children." It was
                   ADVERB

a/an _____ job, but somebody had to do it!
      ADJECTIVE

MAD LIBS® is fun to play with friends, but you can also play it by yourself! To begin with, DO NOT look at the story on the page below. Fill in the blanks on this page with the words called for. Then, using the words you have selected, fill in the blank spaces in the story.

Now you've created your own hilarious MAD LIBS® game!

## LOIS: WIFE, MOTHER, PIANO TEACHER

ADVERB _____

ADJECTIVE _____

NOUN _____

PLURAL NOUN _____

PLURAL NOUN _____

CELEBRITY _____

NOUN _____

NOUN _____

NOUN _____

VERB _____

PLURAL NOUN _____

PLURAL NOUN _____

NOUN _____

NOUN _____

PART OF THE BODY _____

CELEBRITY (FEMALE) _____

ADJECTIVE _____

# MAD LIBS

## LOIS: WIFE, MOTHER, PIANO TEACHER

One of the most _____ asked questions among women
ADVERB

is: "How can I take care of my family, myself, *and* my career

without going _____?" Lois Griffin has nipped this
ADJECTIVE

problem in the _____. Every morning, she wakes her
NOUN

_____ and makes them scrambled _____
PLURAL NOUN                                           PLURAL NOUN

before they leave for _____ High School. She makes sure
CELEBRITY

her husband has a clean _____ to wear and sends him off.
NOUN

Then Lois cleans the entire _____ from top to bottom and
NOUN

prepares for the afternoon's _____ lessons. When her
NOUN

first student shows up, Lois places Stewie in the _____-
VERB

pen. She changes his _____ and feeds him a can of
PLURAL NOUN

strained string _____ between lessons. By the time the
PLURAL NOUN

rest of the family gets home, Lois has money in her _____,
NOUN

a gourmet _____ on the table, and a smile on her
NOUN

_____. Move over, _____—Lois Griffin is the
PART OF THE BODY            CELEBRITY (FEMALE)

most _____ mom on the block!
ADJECTIVE

MAD LIBS® is fun to play with friends, but you can also play it by yourself! To begin with, DO NOT look at the story on the page below. Fill in the blanks on this page with the words called for. Then, using the words you have selected, fill in the blank spaces in the story.

Now you've created your own hilarious MAD LIBS® game!

# CHRIS'S DIET

PLURAL NOUN _____

NOUN _____

TYPE OF FOOD _____

PLURAL NOUN _____

ADJECTIVE _____

CELEBRITY _____

ADJECTIVE _____

PLURAL NOUN _____

PLURAL NOUN _____

PLURAL NOUN _____

PART OF THE BODY _____

NOUN _____

NOUN _____

PLURAL NOUN _____

ADJECTIVE _____

LAST NAME OF CELEBRITY _____

ADJECTIVE _____

PLURAL NOUN _____

# MAD LIBS®

# CHRIS'S DIET

It sure is hard trying to lose weight. So far I've tried Weight

_____, Nutri-_____, and the _____
  PLURAL NOUN                NOUN                   TYPE OF FOOD

Diet. I've lost a couple of _____, but I have to keep at it
                                  PLURAL NOUN

because I want to be as _____ as _____.
                         ADJECTIVE           CELEBRITY

The problem is, the minute I go on a/an _____
                                          ADJECTIVE

diet, I can't stop thinking about all my favorite foods! I crave

chocolate-covered _____ and cheeseburgers with a side
                       PLURAL NOUN

of _____. I want sugar-frosted _____ and
     PLURAL NOUN                          PLURAL NOUN

candies that melt in your mouth—not in your _____. Oh
                                        PART OF THE BODY

man, I just gotta focus on something else besides _____,
                                        NOUN

or I'll never make it through the _____. Maybe I can
                                NOUN

count _____ or draw _____ pictures or
       PLURAL NOUN                 ADJECTIVE

watch *Gumbel to* _____ on TV. I could always do
                     LAST NAME OF CELEBRITY

my _____ homework—but that sounds about as much
    ADJECTIVE

fun as eating _____. Hmm . . . all this thinking is making
           PLURAL NOUN

me hungry—I'm gonna go get a snack!

MAD LIBS® is fun to play with friends, but you can also play it by yourself! To begin with, DO NOT look at the story on the page below. Fill in the blanks on this page with the words called for. Then, using the words you have selected, fill in the blank spaces in the story.

Now you've created your own hilarious MAD LIBS® game!

# THE GUYS

VERB _____

A PLACE _____

VERB ENDING IN "ING" _____

ADJECTIVE _____

ADJECTIVE _____

EXCLAMATION _____

ADJECTIVE _____

NOUN _____

ADVERB _____

NOUN _____

ADVERB _____

NOUN _____

ADVERB _____

A PLACE _____

PLURAL NOUN _____

VERB ENDING IN "ING" _____

ADJECTIVE _____

SILLY WORD _____

# MAD LIBS®
# THE GUYS

Now and then, Peter Griffin and his buddies get together and do

"man things," such as _____ down at the bowling alley and
                          VERB

play baseball at (the) _____. While _____ in
                      A PLACE              VERB ENDING IN "ING"

the Griffins' yard one _____ day, Peter mused, "Isn't it great
                       ADJECTIVE

to be independent and _____ men? We can do whatever we
                      ADJECTIVE

want." "_____!" responded Quagmire. "We're _____
         EXCLAMATION                                   ADJECTIVE

and in charge!" "We're the masters of our _____!" agreed
                                          NOUN

Joe and Cleveland. Just then, Lois opened a window and shouted

_____, "Peter Griffin, get in here and clean out the
   ADVERB

_____ like you said you were gonna do!" _____,
   NOUN                                               ADVERB

Peter said, "Uh . . . gotta go, guys." "I'd better go, too," Cleveland added.

"I need to make more _____ salad at the deli." "Me too," Joe
                     NOUN

said _____. "I'm on duty tonight at (the) _____."
     ADVERB                                          A PLACE

Quagmire headed to the beach to check out the lovely _____.
                                                     PLURAL NOUN

As he was _____, he called out, "Guess you guys aren't as
          VERB ENDING IN "ING"

_____ as me. Giggety, giggety, _____!"
   ADJECTIVE                               SILLY WORD

FROM FAMILY GUY MAD LIBS® • Family Guy TM & © 2007 Twentieth Century Fox Film Corporation. All Rights Reserved. Published by Price Stern Sloan, a division of Penguin Young Readers Group, 345 Hudson Street, New York, New York 10014.

MAD LIBS® is fun to play with friends, but you can also play it by yourself! To begin with, DO NOT look at the story on the page below. Fill in the blanks on this page with the words called for. Then, using the words you have selected, fill in the blank spaces in the story.

Now you've created your own hilarious MAD LIBS® game!

# THE PLIGHT OF BRIAN

ADJECTIVE _____

ADVERB _____

ADJECTIVE _____

CELEBRITY _____

PLURAL NOUN _____

VERB _____

ADVERB _____

SAME VERB _____

NOUN _____

ADJECTIVE _____

ADJECTIVE _____

PLURAL NOUN _____

NOUN _____

ADJECTIVE _____

PART OF THE BODY _____

VERB _____

# MAD LIBS

# THE PLIGHT OF BRIAN

At first I didn't want to be entered in Quahog's 23rd Annual

_____ Dog Show, but when Peter said it was for the good
ADJECTIVE

of the family, I _____ agreed. To prepare, I quickly studied
ADVERB

_____ Shakespeare plays, rehearsed my _____
ADJECTIVE                                                              CELEBRITY

impressions, and even brushed up on my musical _____.
PLURAL NOUN

But when the show started, the emcee came up to me and

commanded, "_____!" I just stared at him _____.
VERB                                                            ADVERB

Why should I _____? I'm not a/an _____.
SAME VERB                                          NOUN

Then he ordered me to roll over and play _____.
ADJECTIVE

Ridiculous. I suddenly realized that this _____ contest was
ADJECTIVE

designed to make dogs look like _____, and I refused to
PLURAL NOUN

continue. I am outraged that Peter, my own best _____,
NOUN

would want me to submit to such _____ commands.
ADJECTIVE

When I get home I'll look him right in the _____ and
PART OF THE BODY

shout, "_____!" just to teach him a lesson. On second
VERB

thought, never mind. He'll probably do it—with enthusiasm, no less.

FROM FAMILY GUY MAD LIBS® • Family Guy TM & © 2007 Twentieth Century Fox Film Corporation.
All Rights Reserved. Published by Price Stern Sloan, a division of Penguin Young Readers Group,
345 Hudson Street, New York, New York 10014.

MAD LIBS® is fun to play with friends, but you can also play it by yourself! To begin with, DO NOT look at the story on the page below. Fill in the blanks on this page with the words called for. Then, using the words you have selected, fill in the blank spaces in the story.

Now you've created your own hilarious MAD LIBS® game!

# "THE DAY PETER AND I MET" BY LOIS

VERB ENDING IN "ING" _____

ADJECTIVE _____

NOUN _____

ADVERB _____

NOUN _____

VERB ENDING IN "ING" _____

ADJECTIVE _____

NOUN _____

OCCUPATION _____

PLURAL NOUN _____

ADVERB _____

PLURAL NOUN _____

ADJECTIVE _____

PLURAL NOUN _____

ADJECTIVE _____

ADJECTIVE _____

PLURAL NOUN _____

# MAD LIBS®

# "THE DAY PETER AND I MET" BY LOIS

Sometimes people look at me and my husband _____
_VERB ENDING IN "ING"_

down the street and think, *What's a/an* _____ *woman*
_ADJECTIVE_

*like Lois doing with a/an* _____ *like him?* They don't
_NOUN_

realize that we happen to be _____ in love. Peter is
_ADVERB_

my _____ in shining armor. The day we met, I was
_NOUN_

coming out of the country club _____ pool and was
_VERB ENDING IN "ING"_

_____ and cold. I needed a/an _____
_ADJECTIVE_ _NOUN_

badly, and I didn't know where to find one. Then, suddenly, there

he was. Peter was the _____ at the pool, and he had
_OCCUPATION_

lots of soft, dry, warm _____ for all the swimmers to
_PLURAL NOUN_

use. I was ever so grateful—and _____ smitten.
_ADVERB_

He made me laugh with his silly _____ and
_PLURAL NOUN_

_____ disposition. Some men shower their wives with
_ADJECTIVE_

pretty _____ while others write _____ poetry.
_PLURAL NOUN_ _ADJECTIVE_

My Peter is just his genuine, honest, _____ self, and
_ADJECTIVE_

that's been enough to keep me head over _____ in love!
_PLURAL NOUN_

FROM FAMILY GUY MAD LIBS® • Family Guy TM & © 2007 Twentieth Century Fox Film Corporation.
All Rights Reserved. Published by Price Stern Sloan, a division of Penguin Young Readers Group,
345 Hudson Street, New York, New York 10014.

MAD LIBS® is fun to play with friends, but you can also play it by yourself! To begin with, DO NOT look at the story on the page below. Fill in the blanks on this page with the words called for. Then, using the words you have selected, fill in the blank spaces in the story.

Now you've created your own hilarious MAD LIBS® game!

## STEWIE'S MASTER PLAN

ADVERB _____

ADJECTIVE _____

NOUN _____

ADJECTIVE _____

VERB ENDING IN "ING" _____

NUMBER_____

NOUN _____

SAME NOUN _____

PLURAL NOUN_____

NOUN _____

PLURAL NOUN_____

PLURAL NOUN_____

ADJECTIVE _____

NOUN _____

PLURAL NOUN_____

PLURAL NOUN_____

SAME PLURAL NOUN _____

ADVERB _____

NOUN _____

# MAD LIBS®

# STEWIE'S MASTER PLAN

I've _____ done it! I've come up with a/an _____
       ADVERB                                              ADJECTIVE

plan to conquer every _____ in the world. I just need a
                              NOUN

few _____ items to make sure everything goes, as they say,
       ADJECTIVE

smooth _____. First, I'll buy a/an _____ mega-
        VERB ENDING IN "ING"                    NUMBER

watt _____-control device from www._____
         NOUN                                      SAME NOUN

controldevices.com. This will force all the _____
                                              PLURAL NOUN

into submission when I give orders like: "Change my dirty

_____!" Next, I'll need one thousand _____
     NOUN                                            PLURAL NOUN

to pay for _____ and other _____
              PLURAL NOUN                  ADJECTIVE

materials. It also helps to have extra money in case a sudden

_____ arises. Finally, I need a squad of trained
       NOUN

_____ to launch _____ into the air on my
   PLURAL NOUN                 PLURAL NOUN

command. People are defenseless against flying _____.
                                                 SAME PLURAL NOUN

They will surrender _____, and I will rule over this
                         ADVERB

puny little _____ once and for all!
                  NOUN

MAD LIBS® is fun to play with friends, but you can also play it by yourself! To begin with, DO NOT look at the story on the page below. Fill in the blanks on this page with the words called for. Then, using the words you have selected, fill in the blank spaces in the story.

Now you've created your own hilarious MAD LIBS® game!

# GRIFFIN FAMILY CHRISTMAS

PLURAL NOUN _____

A PLACE _____

NOUN _____

NOUN _____

PLURAL NOUN _____

CELEBRITY _____

NOUN _____

ADJECTIVE _____

NOUN _____

NOUN _____

ADJECTIVE _____

PLURAL NOUN _____

PLURAL NOUN _____

ADJECTIVE _____

ADJECTIVE _____

EXCLAMATION _____

ADJECTIVE _____

NOUN _____

NOUN _____

# MAD LIBS®

# GRIFFIN FAMILY CHRISTMAS

Year after year, the Griffins observe the same Christmas

_____. Peter goes out to (the) _____ and
PLURAL NOUN                         A PLACE

chops down a fresh pine _____ to place in the living
NOUN

_____. The kids hang _____ over the
NOUN                       PLURAL NOUN

fireplace, hoping that _____ will fill them with candy.
CELEBRITY

Lois puts a delicious roast on the _____ before taking
NOUN

Stewie to the _____ shopping _____ to sit
ADJECTIVE                  NOUN

on Santa's _____. The Griffins also help the "less
NOUN

_____" children of the world by donating several
ADJECTIVE

_____ to _____ for Tots. And what
PLURAL NOUN        PLURAL NOUN

would the holidays be without lots and lots of _____
ADJECTIVE

toys? The Griffins aren't afraid to fight like crazed _____
ADJECTIVE

warriors for the best ones. _____! Peter just tripped
EXCLAMATION

a/an _____ lady so he could get the last toy
ADJECTIVE

_____ for Stewie. That's the holiday _____
NOUN                            NOUN

for you—Griffin-style!

MAD LIBS® is fun to play with friends, but you can also play it by yourself! To begin with, DO NOT look at the story on the page below. Fill in the blanks on this page with the words called for. Then, using the words you have selected, fill in the blank spaces in the story.

Now you've created your own hilarious MAD LIBS® game!

## NEIGHBORS

PLURAL NOUN _____

ADJECTIVE _____

VERB _____

ADJECTIVE _____

NOUN _____

ADJECTIVE _____

A PLACE _____

ADJECTIVE _____

PLURAL NOUN _____

ADJECTIVE _____

VERB ENDING IN "ING" _____

NOUN _____

PLURAL NOUN _____

ADJECTIVE _____

NOUN _____

# NEIGHBORS

The _____ who live on Spooner Street make it a/an
　　　　PLURAL NOUN

_____ place to _____. When Joe and his family
　　ADJECTIVE　　　　　　　　　　VERB

came to Quahog, Bonnie and Lois became _____ friends,
　　　　　　　　　　　　　　　　　　　　　　　ADJECTIVE

and Joe helped Peter's company win a/an _____-ball game.
　　　　　　　　　　　　　　　　　　　　　　　NOUN

And then there's Cleveland, whose _____ nature brings
　　　　　　　　　　　　　　　　　　　ADJECTIVE

warmth and sensitivity to the group. Plus he has the finest mustache

in (the) _____. Another neighbor, Quagmire, is always ready
　　　　　A PLACE

to have a/an _____ time. But even mature _____
　　　　　　ADJECTIVE　　　　　　　　　　　　　　PLURAL NOUN

can get a little _____ with each other. One time, Peter felt
　　　　　　　ADJECTIVE

jealous that his family seemed to like _____ with Joe
　　　　　　　　　　　　　　　　　VERB ENDING IN "ING"

more than with him. On another occasion, Peter ruined Cleveland's

chances of appearing on the reality TV show *The* _____.
　　　　　　　　　　　　　　　　　　　　　　　　　NOUN

And Lois really got angry when Quagmire stole her _____.
　　　　　　　　　　　　　　　　　　　　　　　　PLURAL NOUN

Still, they all manage to live in harmony. That's what being a/an

_____ neighbor is all about—putting up with people
　　ADJECTIVE

who drive you up the _____!
　　　　　　　　　　NOUN

MAD LIBS® is fun to play with friends, but you can also play it by yourself! To begin with, DO NOT look at the story on the page below. Fill in the blanks on this page with the words called for. Then, using the words you have selected, fill in the blank spaces in the story.

Now you've created your own hilarious MAD LIBS® game!

# NO TV

ADJECTIVE _____

ADJECTIVE _____

NOUN _____

PLURAL NOUN _____

NOUN _____

PART OF THE BODY (PLURAL) _____

NOUN _____

NOUN _____

EXCLAMATION _____

VERB ENDING IN "ING" _____

ADJECTIVE _____

ADJECTIVE _____

ADJECTIVE _____

ADJECTIVE _____

NOUN _____

ADVERB _____

PLURAL NOUN _____

PERSON IN ROOM _____

NOUN _____

ADVERB _____

NOUN _____

# MAD LIBS®

# NO TV

It was a dark and _____ night. Peter Griffin had returned
　　　　　　　　　　　ADJECTIVE

home from a/an _____ day at the _____
　　　　　　　　　　ADJECTIVE　　　　　　　　　　　NOUN

and kicked off his _____. He sat down on his favorite
　　　　　　　　　　PLURAL NOUN

_____, put his _____ up on the
　　　　NOUN　　　　　　　　　　PART OF THE BODY (PLURAL)

_____, clicked the remote _____ . . . and nothing
　　NOUN　　　　　　　　　　　　　　　NOUN

happened. "_____!" he shrieked. The rest of the family
　　　　　　EXCLAMATION

came _____ into the room. "What?!" they asked. Then
　　VERB ENDING IN "ING"

they saw the _____ screen and responded in horror,
　　　　　　ADJECTIVE

"Nooooooo!!!" "Wait a minute, everyone. Stay _____!" Lois
　　　　　　　　　　　　　　　　　　　　　ADJECTIVE

instructed. "The batteries are probably _____, that's all.
　　　　　　　　　　　　　　　　ADJECTIVE

Brian, go get some _____ ones from the _____
　　　　　　　　ADJECTIVE　　　　　　　　　　　　NOUN

upstairs. And go _____—it's almost primetime!" Within
　　　　　　　ADVERB

seconds, Brian returned with new _____ and Lois had
　　　　　　　　　　　　　PLURAL NOUN

the remote working again. The television was on in time for their

favorite show, _____ *and the* _____. "Aw, Lois,"
　　　　　PERSON IN ROOM　　　　　　　　　NOUN

Peter said _____, "you saved the _____ again!"
　　　　　ADVERB　　　　　　　　　　　NOUN

MAD LIBS® is fun to play with friends, but you can also play it by yourself! To begin with, DO NOT look at the story on the page below. Fill in the blanks on this page with the words called for. Then, using the words you have selected, fill in the blank spaces in the story.

Now you've created your own hilarious MAD LIBS® game!

## THOSE PESKY RELATIVES

ADJECTIVE _____

ADVERB _____

NOUN _____

ADJECTIVE _____

NOUN _____

ADJECTIVE _____

ADJECTIVE _____

PLURAL NOUN_____

NUMBER_____

PLURAL NOUN_____

VERB ENDING IN "ING" _____

NOUN _____

NOUN _____

ADJECTIVE _____

PLURAL NOUN_____

NOUN _____

# MAD LIBS®

# THOSE PESKY RELATIVES

Every family has one or two _____ relatives they don't
ADJECTIVE

get along _____ with, and the Griffins are no exception.
ADVERB

Peter's father, Francis, is not very affectionate. He's always telling

Peter how to live his _____. He is also fond of calling
NOUN

Lois a/an _____ _____. Lois's parents, Carter
ADJECTIVE          NOUN

and Babs Pewterschmidt, are just as _____. They only
ADJECTIVE

care about _____ yachts, five-star _____,
ADJECTIVE                              PLURAL NOUN

and _____-carat gold _____. Not only
NUMBER                        PLURAL NOUN

that, but Mr. Pewterschmidt once forbid Lois to pursue a career in

_____, even though that was what she wanted
VERB ENDING IN "ING"

most in the whole wide _____. As for Lois's brother,
NOUN

Patrick, well—he has an imaginary _____. The Griffins
NOUN

are just happy that he's back at the home for _____
ADJECTIVE

_____, and learning to deal with his _____ in a
PLURAL NOUN                                      NOUN

healthy way.

MAD LIBS® is fun to play with friends, but you can also play it by yourself! To begin with, DO NOT look at the story on the page below. Fill in the blanks on this page with the words called for. Then, using the words you have selected, fill in the blank spaces in the story.

Now you've created your own hilarious MAD LIBS® game!

## PETER'S VALENTINE'S DAY GIFT FOR LOIS

NOUN _____

ADJECTIVE _____

PLURAL NOUN _____

CELEBRITY _____

ADJECTIVE _____

VERB (PAST TENSE) _____

PLURAL NOUN _____

VERB ENDING IN "ING" _____

ADJECTIVE _____

EXCLAMATION _____

ADJECTIVE _____

ADJECTIVE _____

NOUN _____

ADJECTIVE _____

NOUN _____

PLURAL NOUN _____

# MAD LIBS®
# PETER'S VALENTINE'S DAY GIFT FOR LOIS

Aw geez—Valentine's Day is just around the _____,
                                                    NOUN

and I haven't gotten Lois a gift yet. She deserves something extra-

_____ this year—not just the usual bouquet of
        ADJECTIVE

_____ .What's more, for our anniversary last year I had
    PLURAL NOUN

_____ perform a special concert just for us, and I don't
     CELEBRITY

know if I can top that! Maybe I should get her a gift certificate to a/an

_____ spa, where she can get her back _____
        ADJECTIVE                                    VERB (PAST TENSE)

with hot _____ .That would help her to relax, which she
          PLURAL NOUN

needs after a long day of _____ at home and putting up
                          VERB ENDING IN "ING"

with my _____ antics. Or, hmm, let's see, diamonds? No.
          ADJECTIVE

Fur coat? Nah. Perfume? Blech. A Galaga machine? _____ !
                                                        EXCLAMATION

That's it! Man, that was my favorite _____ arcade game
                                        ADJECTIVE

back in the day! I could play that thing for hours! I even had the high

score at the _____ _____ Arcade. A Galaga
                ADJECTIVE        NOUN

machine will make Lois's whole day as bright and _____
                                                      ADJECTIVE

as a summer's _____ ! But I call first _____ !
                NOUN                                 PLURAL NOUN

MAD LIBS® is fun to play with friends, but you can also play it by yourself! To begin with, DO NOT look at the story on the page below. Fill in the blanks on this page with the words called for. Then, using the words you have selected, fill in the blank spaces in the story.

Now you've created your own hilarious MAD LIBS® game!

# QUAHOG 5 NEWS

PLURAL NOUN_____

OCCUPATION_____

PERSON IN ROOM _____

VERB ENDING IN "ING"_____

ADJECTIVE _____

NUMBER_____

PLURAL NOUN_____

VERB _____

PLURAL NOUN_____

VERB ENDING IN "ING"_____

ADJECTIVE _____

NOUN _____

PERSON IN ROOM (FEMALE) _____

VERB ENDING IN "ING"_____

ADJECTIVE _____

SAME PERSON IN ROOM _____

PLURAL NOUN_____

ADJECTIVE _____

# MAD LIBS

# QUAHOG 5 NEWS

Good afternoon, ladies and _____, we're Tricia
_____(PLURAL NOUN)

Takanawa, Tom Tucker, and Diane Simmons and this is the

*Quahog 5 News.* This morning, a/an _____ by the name
_____(OCCUPATION)

of _____ was arrested for _____ recklessly
(PERSON IN ROOM) (VERB ENDING IN "ING")

in the _____ parking lot of a local _____/11.
(ADJECTIVE) (NUMBER)

Police took the perpetrator into custody, thus assuring the safety

of innocent _____ everywhere. In other news, Mayor
(PLURAL NOUN)

West has declared today the first annual "Quahog _____
(VERB)

Day," so get out your _____ and start _____
(PLURAL NOUN) (VERB ENDING IN "ING")

away, citizens! Finally, a/an _____ _____
(ADJECTIVE) (NOUN)

by the name of _____ made Quahog history this
(PERSON IN ROOM (FEMALE))

afternoon. At approximately 3:36 P.M., she broke the record for

most consecutive hours spent _____ on one leg.
(VERB ENDING IN "ING")

Congratulations on your _____ achievement,
(ADJECTIVE)

_____. It's _____ like you who really
(SAME PERSON IN ROOM) (PLURAL NOUN)

make Quahog the _____ place it is!
(ADJECTIVE)

FROM FAMILY GUY MAD LIBS® • Family Guy TM & © 2007 Twentieth Century Fox Film Corporation.
All Rights Reserved. Published by Price Stern Sloan, a division of Penguin Young Readers Group,
345 Hudson Street, New York, New York 10014.

MAD LIBS® is fun to play with friends, but you can also play it by yourself! To begin with, DO NOT look at the story on the page below. Fill in the blanks on this page with the words called for. Then, using the words you have selected, fill in the blank spaces in the story.

Now you've created your own hilarious MAD LIBS® game!

---

## "FOR LOVE OR MONEY" BY LOIS

ADJECTIVE _____

NOUN _____

NOUN _____

PLURAL NOUN_____

OCCUPATION_____

NOUN _____

VERB ENDING IN "ING"_____

NOUN _____

VERB ENDING IN "ING"_____

ADJECTIVE _____

PLURAL NOUN_____

ADVERB _____

PLURAL NOUN_____

ADJECTIVE _____

NOUN _____

NOUN _____

NOUN _____

ADJECTIVE _____

NOUN _____

A PLACE_____

VERB ENDING IN "ING"_____

# MAD LIBS®

# "FOR LOVE OR MONEY" BY LOIS

When I was a/an _____ little girl, my parents expected
                    ADJECTIVE

me to marry a Harvard _____. They envisioned me
                        NOUN

with a/an _____ executive who would make a fortune
          NOUN

selling _____, or maybe with a/an _____ who
        PLURAL NOUN                            OCCUPATION

would build our nest _____ by _____ on
                      NOUN                VERB ENDING IN "ING"

Wall Street. Instead, I married Peter Griffin, the _____ boy
                                                    NOUN

at our country club's _____ pool. Peter is not wealthy,
                       VERB ENDING IN "ING"

or _____. My father even offered Peter one million
    ADJECTIVE

_____ to *not* marry me! But Peter _____ turned
PLURAL NOUN                                    ADVERB

him down, and do you know why? Because he's got something that

none of those Harvard _____ have—a/an _____
                       PLURAL NOUN                ADJECTIVE

_____. Sometimes he behaves like a/an _____,
NOUN                                              NOUN

but I love that he's honest and always says exactly what's on his

_____. Plus, I love his _____ sense of humor and
NOUN                                ADJECTIVE

cute _____. So maybe I won't be living in a castle in (the)
      NOUN

_____, but at least I've got a true Prince _____!
A PLACE                                                VERB ENDING IN "ING"

MAD LIBS® is fun to play with friends, but you can also play it by yourself! To begin with, DO NOT look at the story on the page below. Fill in the blanks on this page with the words called for. Then, using the words you have selected, fill in the blank spaces in the story.

Now you've created your own hilarious MAD LIBS® game!

# DAY CARE

ADJECTIVE _____

PLURAL NOUN _____

ADJECTIVE _____

PLURAL NOUN _____

NOUN _____

ADJECTIVE _____

PERSON IN ROOM (MALE) _____

NOUN _____

ADJECTIVE _____

PART OF THE BODY _____

LAST NAME OF PERSON _____

ADJECTIVE _____

NOUN _____

ADJECTIVE _____

NOUN _____

NOUN _____

NOUN _____

# MAD LIBS®
# DAY CARE

Lois, that _____ woman, has had me committed to
<br>ADJECTIVE

a toddler germ factory called Hugs and _____ Day
<br>PLURAL NOUN

Care Center. It is a vile place full of _____ children
<br>ADJECTIVE

who have nothing but _____ between their ears.
<br>PLURAL NOUN

Just this morning I was playing "_____ on the Orient
<br>NOUN

Express" when a/an _____ little boy by the name of
<br>ADJECTIVE

_____ picked up my train and put it in his
<br>PERSON IN ROOM (MALE)

_____. He then slobbered all over it and ruined my
<br>NOUN

_____ tale of intrigue and mystery. So, naturally, I stuck
<br>ADJECTIVE

my _____ out at him. Ms. _____,
<br>PART OF THE BODY      LAST NAME OF PERSON

the evil overseer of this _____ prison, came over and
<br>ADJECTIVE

said, "Bad! Bad Stewie!" and she placed me in the _____
<br>NOUN

for a time out! I shan't be treated like some _____
<br>ADJECTIVE

_____! Someday I shall become supreme _____
<br>NOUN        NOUN

of the entire _____ and then we'll see who's boss,
<br>NOUN

hmm? Then we'll see who needs a time out!

MAD LIBS® is fun to play with friends, but you can also play it by yourself! To begin with, DO NOT look at the story on the page below. Fill in the blanks on this page with the words called for. Then, using the words you have selected, fill in the blank spaces in the story.

Now you've created your own hilarious MAD LIBS® game!

---

## "LIFE WITH THE GRIFFINS" BY BRIAN

ADJECTIVE _____

VERB _____

NOUN _____

PLURAL NOUN _____

PLURAL NOUN _____

NOUN _____

OCCUPATION _____

VERB _____

NOUN _____

ADJECTIVE _____

ADJECTIVE _____

NOUN _____

PART OF THE BODY _____

NOUN _____

VERB (PAST TENSE) _____

NOUN _____

ADVERB _____

NOUN _____

# MAD LIBS
# "LIFE WITH THE GRIFFINS"
# BY BRIAN

Peter Griffin, despite being such a/an _____ doofus, is my
ADJECTIVE

best friend. When I was homeless, Peter took me in. Now I have a

warm place to _____ at night and a loving _____
VERB                                    NOUN

to call my own. Lois and I have conversations about everything

from _____ to _____. She once directed
PLURAL NOUN          PLURAL NOUN

the play *The* _____ *and I* and gave me the part of the
NOUN

_____. I hope we can _____ together again in
OCCUPATION                    VERB

the future. Stewie is kind of a pain in the _____—a little too
NOUN

_____ and _____ for my taste. Chris isn't the
ADJECTIVE            ADJECTIVE

brightest _____ on the block, but his _____
NOUN                                PART OF THE BODY

is always in the right place. Meg is . . . uh . . . what can I say about

Meg? She's, uh . . . Meg has a very nice _____. Wait, no she
NOUN

doesn't, let me try that again. Meg has never _____ on a
VERB (PAST TENSE)

stage while singing and wearing a/an _____ costume. For
NOUN

that I am _____ grateful. I wouldn't trade my life with the
ADVERB

Griffins for anything . . . except a/an _____ . . . maybe.
NOUN

MAD LIBS® is fun to play with friends, but you can also play it by yourself! To begin with, DO NOT look at the story on the page below. Fill in the blanks on this page with the words called for. Then, using the words you have selected, fill in the blank spaces in the story.

Now you've created your own hilarious MAD LIBS® game!

# "WHAT DOES IT TAKE TO BE POPULAR?" BY MEG GRIFFIN

ADJECTIVE _____

PLURAL NOUN _____

SILLY WORD _____

NOUN _____

NOUN _____

PLURAL NOUN _____

NOUN _____

SAME NOUN _____

VERB ENDING IN "ING" _____

PLURAL NOUN _____

VERB ENDING IN "ING" _____

ADJECTIVE _____

NOUN _____

PERSON IN ROOM _____

PLURAL NOUN _____

VERB _____

VERB (PAST TENSE) _____

# MAD LIBS
# "WHAT DOES IT TAKE TO BE POPULAR?" BY MEG GRIFFIN

In order to be _____ at my school, you have to follow
ADJECTIVE

certain _____. If you're a girl, you need a/an _____
PLURAL NOUN                                              SILLY WORD

purse. If you're a guy, you need to drive a fancy _____.
NOUN

Even though this stuff costs an arm and a/an _____, all
NOUN

the cool _____ have them. Second, if you're a girl, you're
PLURAL NOUN

supposed to date the captain of the _____ team, or at
NOUN

least a/an _____ player. If you're a guy, you have to date the
SAME NOUN

captain of the cheer-_____ squad. And, no matter who
VERB ENDING IN "ING"

you are, you have to choose the right _____ to hang out
PLURAL NOUN

with. Under no circumstances can you be caught _____
VERB ENDING IN "ING"

with a/an _____ _____ or even talking to a
ADJECTIVE          NOUN

nerd like _____. Just being around these _____
PERSON IN ROOM                                        PLURAL NOUN

will damage your reputation and you'll have to _____
VERB

alone in the cafeteria for weeks! Trust me, I know. Becoming popular

is easier said than _____!
VERB (PAST TENSE)

FROM FAMILY GUY MAD LIBS® • Family Guy TM & © 2007 Twentieth Century Fox Film Corporation.
All Rights Reserved. Published by Price Stern Sloan, a division of Penguin Young Readers Group,
345 Hudson Street, New York, New York 10014.

MAD LIBS® is fun to play with friends, but you can also play it by yourself! To begin with, DO NOT look at the story on the page below. Fill in the blanks on this page with the words called for. Then, using the words you have selected, fill in the blank spaces in the story.

Now you've created your own hilarious MAD LIBS® game!

## BRIAN AND STEWIE GO TO . . .

ADJECTIVE _____

NOUN _____

NOUN _____

NOUN _____

PLURAL NOUN _____

EXCLAMATION _____

NOUN _____

PLURAL NOUN _____

ADVERB _____

ADJECTIVE _____

PLURAL NOUN _____

OCCUPATION _____

SAME PLURAL NOUN _____

VERB ENDING IN "ING" _____

NOUN _____

ADJECTIVE _____

NOUN _____

ADJECTIVE _____

# MAD LIBS

# BRIAN AND STEWIE GO TO . . .

At the end of a visit with Stewie's _____ grandparents,
<small>ADJECTIVE</small>

Brian and Stewie took a/an _____ to the airport only to find
<small>NOUN</small>

their _____ was delayed. They decided to go by _____
<small>NOUN</small> <small>NOUN</small>

instead, but the driver looked at them and said, "No _____
<small>PLURAL NOUN</small>

allowed." "_____!" Stewie said and squirted him with his
<small>EXCLAMATION</small>

super-powered water-_____. "Hold your _____,
<small>NOUN</small> <small>PLURAL NOUN</small>

Stewie," Brian said _____. "I've got another idea." He
<small>ADVERB</small>

dragged Stewie to a field full of _____ hot-air balloons.
<small>ADJECTIVE</small>

"Tickets cost fifty _____," said the balloon _____.
<small>PLURAL NOUN</small> <small>OCCUPATION</small>

"But we don't have any _____," Brian pleaded. "Is there
<small>SAME PLURAL NOUN</small>

some other way we can pay?" Within minutes, Brian and Stewie were

tap-_____ and singing along to the tune of "Alexander's
<small>VERB ENDING IN "ING"</small>

Ragtime _____." The balloonist clapped. "You guys are
<small>NOUN</small>

really _____," he said. "I'll take you anywhere you want!"
<small>ADJECTIVE</small>

Brian and Stewie rode the hot-_____ balloon and flew all
<small>NOUN</small>

the way back to Quahog—home, _____ home!
<small>ADJECTIVE</small>

This book is published by

*PSS!*

PRICE STERN SLOAN

**whose other splendid titles include such literary classics as**

The Original #1 Mad Libs®

Son of Mad Libs®

Sooper Dooper Mad Libs®

Monster Mad Libs®

Goofy Mad Libs®

Off-the-Wall Mad Libs®

Vacation Fun Mad Libs®

Camp Daze Mad Libs®

Christmas Fun Mad Libs®

Mad Libs® 40th Anniversary Deluxe Edition

Mad Mad Mad Mad Mad Libs®

Mad Libs® On the Road

The Apprentice™ Mad Libs®

Austin Powers™ Mad Libs®

The Powerpuff Girls™ Mad Libs®

Scooby-Doo!™ Mad Libs®

Scooby-Doo!™ Mystery Mad Libs®

Scooby-Doo!™ Movie Mad Libs®

Operation™ Mad Libs®

SpongeBob SquarePants™ Mad Libs®

Fear Factor™ Mad Libs®

Fear Factor™ Mad Libs®: Ultimate Gross Out!

Survivor™ Mad Libs®

Guinness World Records™ Mad Libs®

Betty and Veronica® Mad Libs®

Napoleon Dynamite™ Mad Libs®

Nancy Drew® Mad Libs®

The Mad Libs® Worst-Case Scenario™ Survival Handbook

The Mad Libs® Worst-Case Scenario™ Survival Handbook 2

The Mad Libs® Worst-Case Scenario Survival Handbook™: Travel

The Mad Libs® Worst-Case Scenario Survival Handbook™: Holidays

**and many, many more!**

**Mad Libs® are available wherever books are sold.**